Jungle Tales

NATRAJ PUBLISHERS
17, Rajpur Road, DEHRADUN

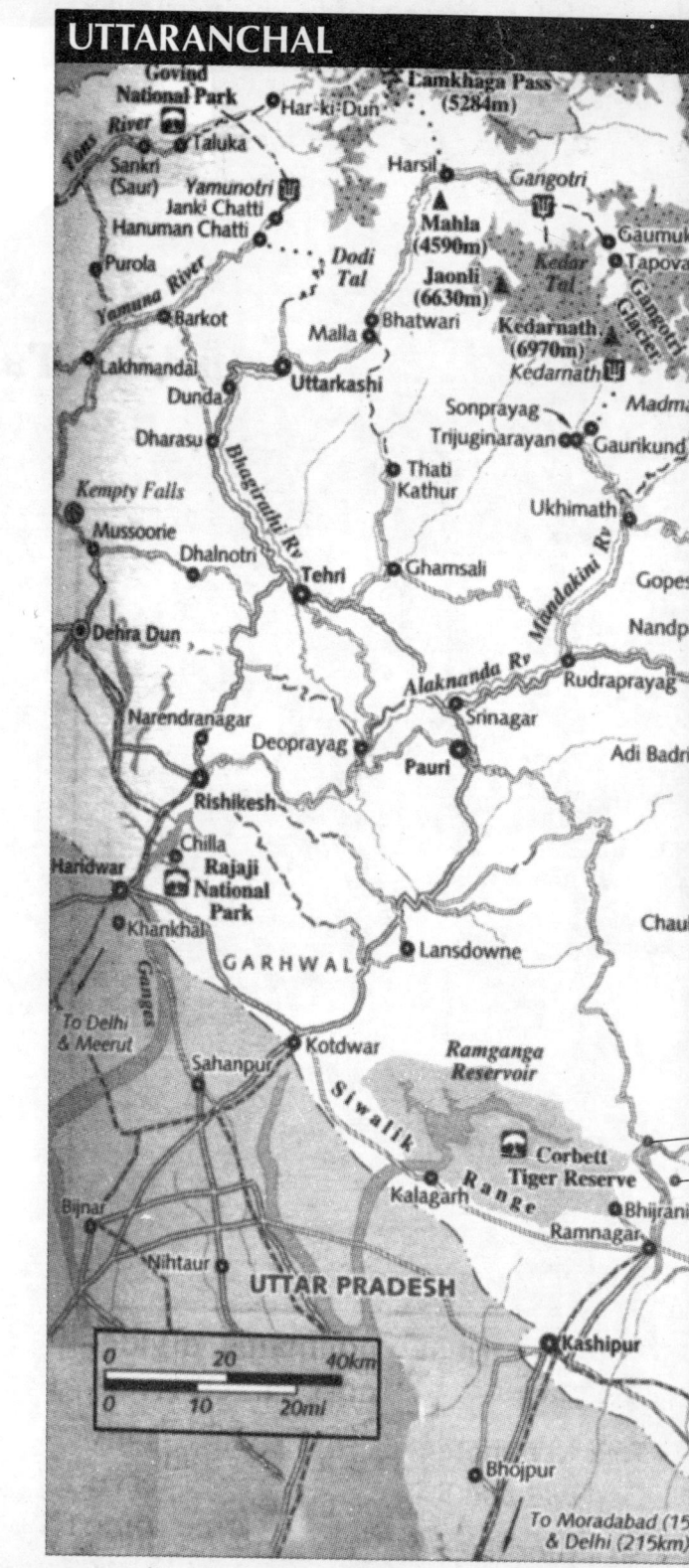

Other Story Books by UNICORN

80/-

80/-

68/-

68/-

80/-

80/-

Postage: Rs. 15/- each book. Every subsequent book: Rs. 5/- extra.

JUNGLE TALES

*The author's thrilling account of his adventures on the
trail of legendary Jim Corbett and the man-eaters he shot*

Joel Lyall

UNICORN

Publishers
UNICORN BOOKS Pvt. Ltd.
J-3/16, Daryaganj, New Delhi-110002
☎ 23276539, 23272783, 23272784 • *Fax:* 011-23260518
E-mail: unicornbooks@vsnl.com
Website: www.unicornbooks.in • www.kidscorner.in

Distributors
Pustak Mahal, Delhi
Bangalore *e-mail:* pmblr@sancharnet.in • pustak@sancharnet.in
Mumbai *e-mail:* rapidex@bom5.vsnl.net.in
Patna *e-mail:* rapidexptn@rediffmail.com
Hyderabad *e-mail:* pustakmahalhyd@yahoo.co.in

© **Copyright : Unicorn Books**

ISBN 81-780-6110-4

Edition : 2006

The Copyright © of this book as well as all matter contained herein (including illustrations) rests with UNICORN BOOKS PVT. LTD. No person shall copy the name of the book, its title design, matter and illustrations in any form and in any language, totally or partially or in any distorted form. Anybody doing so shall face legal action and will be responsible for damages.

Printed at: Unique Color Carton, New Delhi-110064.

Contents

Introduction 09
The Law of Jungle 13
Jungle Lore 17
The Bachelor of Thola Kot 20
The Drongo's Perfect Signal 24
Chuka: The Tigers' Heartland 27
Poacher's Delight 31
Kaladhunga Forest Bungalow 34
A Visit to Sanouli 38
The Temple and the Tiger 41
A Night of Terror 45
The Man who Fought a Tigress 48
My Friend Goonga 52
The Brave Widow of Thak 55
Tryst with a Tigress 59
Old Man and the Forest 62

On a Man-eater's Trail   66

Mysterious Forest Lights   69

Bachelor Boy   74

Muktesar's Man-eater   77

Mystery of the Yeti   80

Corbett's Brave Companion   84

Lights in the Sky   88

How Green was My Valley!   91

Poaching Poses Threat to Wildlife   94

Don't Kill the World...   98

King Bandit   102

Tigers of Talla Des   105

Braving a Bear Attack   108

Jungle Laws are Eternal and True   111

Saluting Some Unsung Jungle Heroes   115

Introduction

My house was surrounded by forest, where game was found in plenty. Naturally, forest became my second playground, a paradise of experience and a sheer heaven. Consequently, all denizens of the forest became my friends.

Later on, I began to learn more and more about those places where the man-eating tigers and leopards killed hundreds of people and established a reign of terror in this part of the country, now known all over the world as Uttaranchal. I, therefore, decided to visit those places where these man-eaters lived, and see with my own eyes and photograph those exact spots where they had been shot. Perseverance and hard work has no substitute. After making painstaking efforts and spending many days and nights all alone in the dense forest, I became the first Indian journalist to have visited and photographed those very places where real action had taken place. The forests of Uttaranchal, therefore, form the backdrop of my narratives.

Forests are the lungs of the world. They contain some of the most vibrant ecosystems on the planet; they are home to a wondrous variety of birds, animals, insects and plants. Every bird, animal and insect has its allotted place in the scheme of nature, which it performs with regularity and precision. As the sun rises in the east, all the birds of the forest, which have a song to sing, sing it to the glory of God. Birds like bulbuls, parrots, peacocks, and orioles beautify nature. Sibias, koels, parakeets, robins, skylarks and nightingales fill nature with melody. Hawks, eagles, crows and falcons keep balance in nature. Animals like deer, langurs, monkeys and antelopes beautify nature, while tigers, leopards, jackals and bears help in maintaining the balance. In nature, there is neither repining nor sorrow. They toil not, nor do they spin, yet they are all happy.

My main aim in writing this book is to create awareness in the minds of people about the role of ecology, and champion the cause of nature to the world which is oblivious to the beauty and wonders of the animal kingdom. The knowledge of the jungle can't be absorbed at a go; it is a lifelong process. As I am reaching the sunset of my life, I feel I have learnt nothing from nature, for the whole nature is before me to be explored.

Alas! the market forces in their greed to make a quick buck are felling trees mercilessly, destroying the habitats of millions of species, sending them to the verge of extinction. If we fail to raise our fingers against the ecocide and the killing of these beautiful animals such as tigers and leopards, it is possible that these species may be wiped out, and eventually become a part of history books or museums.

Lastly, the book mirrors my lifelong association with forest and wildlife, especially the forests of Bhabar and Terai area where once game roamed at will, and tigers and leopards were found in large numbers. First, you reach the town of Tanakpur, and ten kilometres away is Thulighat. From here, a goat track strewn with boulders and passing along the bank of the Sarda river takes you to Chuka village via Kaladhunga forest bungalow. Four kilometres in the south-east and on the bank of the Ladhya river is the place where the Chuka man-eater was shot. A little away in the east of ıka is Thak village where the Thak man-eater killed. From Tanakpur go to Champawat, now trict headquarter. In the east of Champawat is ⅃awra village. Here Gopal Singh Vohar, the *pradhan* and my old friend, will show you the spot where the man-eater of Champawat was sent to the happy hunting grounds. Around twenty kilometres away is Thola Kot village. Convey my regards to Sundar Singh and he will show you the *wyran* field and the place where the Talla Des man-eater was shot. On reaching Almora, go to Panwalona village, climb two ridges, cross the Panar river and you are in the domain of the Panar man-eater, who had killed more than 400 human beings in this area before falling to the gun shots of Jim Corbett. About twenty kilometres away from the town of Ramnagar is Mohan, and around fifteen kilometres away is the village Katkanoula, where Munshi Ram (if alive), will show you the place the Mohan man-eater was killed.

My heart goes out to all those simple, honest and poor people of the forest with whom I spent many happy days of my life and who provided me with a rich mine of information. It is these brave village folk of my country without whose cooperation my mission and work would have been incomplete.

❏❏❏

1

The Law of Jungle

After playing hide-and-seek with Kanda, once a favourite hunting spot of Lord Hailey and a preferred haunt of holiday-makers, the Ramganga river slips into the well-wooded dale of Kalagarh. A few kilometres down from Kalagarh to the west is the Ramganga forest.

On a baking hot day in 1961, I reached this place on a fishing expedition. This part of the river is famed for *mahaseer*.

I stayed in a cottage in a small clearing surrounded by scrub jungle. Close by lived Umed Singh, a veteran of World War II, with his pup of uncertain pedigree. The camaraderie between us was instant.

One late afternoon, on the persistent prodding of Umed Singh, I took my fishing rods and together we headed for the river, dutifully followed by the pup.

Ramganga river near Kalagarh

Sitting on an outcrop of rock and enjoying the cigarettes which I passed on to him, Umed Singh regaled me with stories of his many brave deeds in the war and in the forest, including his hand-to-hand fight with a bear. He proudly showed me a bullet mark on his body which he received while fighting against the Nazis, a scar he would proudly carry till his death, as well as the deep gashes the bear had left on his shoulders.

By the evening we had caught five large fish, sufficient for our pot. The fishing had been good and the view down the Ramganga simply breathtaking. As the shadows lengthened and evening closed in, all the birds of the forest burst into a full-throated song. Just as the symphony reached its crescendo, a spine-chilling call of a tiger came from up the rock cliff facing us. It was time for us to move.

We gathered our catch and rods and began to walk back home. All of a sudden we noticed the pup was missing. Finding it nowhere around, we dashed to the track leading to the cottage. We had hardly gone a short distance through the woods, when I froze at an amazing sight: the pup was trotting behind and trying to snuggle up to a leopard, blissfully ignorant in its innocence that a dog is a favourite dish for the leopard.

Having padded a few steps farther, the leopard whipped round and looked intently at the pup as if to thank the little fellow for its convivial company. And then in one swift, graceful move the leopard was gone into the thicket of brush.

The leopard, Umed Singh told me later, was a full-grown adult which had lived in the vicinity of his cottage for long, but without ever trying to harm him or his pup.

After the lapse of so many years, the gentle leopard and the little pup must surely have departed to meet their Maker. But the true witness to this thrilling incident is still around to mull over the most important lesson he learnt in the jungle: Never kill wantonly, and spare the young of any species for that is where all future life lies. Man has a lot to learn from the savage beasts of the forest.

❑❑❑

2

Jungle Lore

My house was on the edge of the forest. Beyond it lay wilderness and a thickly wooded valley where we could hear the call of the tiger, leopard, barking deer and sambhar. This place was also an ideal meeting ground for highwaymen and bootleggers who were afraid of none save an old Anglo-Indian forest guard who always carried a thick cane, which was twice his height and wore smooth because of its constant collision with human bodies.

As the years rolled by, I got friendly with two brothers: Chattoo and Tilwa. Chattoo was a young man of limited means but unlimited infirmities: from bent legs to one eye that was half shut. His only means of livelihood was to collect fuel wood from the forest and sell it in the market. He was a sworn enemy of the forest guard who could never catch him in the forest despite his best efforts. His younger brother, Tilwa, was an ace hunter. The latter was in the good books of the village *pradhan* whose gun he used liberally to shoot red jungle fowls and rabbits for the family pot.

In those boyhood days, I frequently went deep into the jungle in the company of Tilwa. Being an expert tree climber, my duty was to climb high in the tree and keep an eye out for the forest guard, while Tilwa would go on his errands.

One afternoon, while I was up on a *kafal* tree enjoying its fruit, arrived the forest guard as silently as a shadow. "You little wretch, what are you doing here in the forest?" he asked. "Sir, I am eating *kafal* fruit," I meekly replied. "Then drop some fruit for me too," he sternly ordered, and I dutifully obliged.

Having stuffed his pockets with fruit, he trained his polished axe at me and thundered, "If I see you again in the forest, I will cut you into pieces." A sudden dread possessed me and I felt a pain in my stomach. Fortunately, Tilwa returned safely without being seen or caught by the forest guard. I told him about the incident and we thanked our stars for the narrow escape.

One evening, while I was sitting under a *jamun* tree absorbed in school homework, Tilwa's uncle came to announce his nephew's sudden death due to snake bite. I was deeply saddened, but took heart that Tilwa had returned to happier hunting grounds, far from the shrinking forests in this world.

❑❑❑

3

The Bachelor of **Thola Kot**

All man-eaters and cattle lifters, be they tigers or leopards, are known by the area in which they operate. In this case, it was a young male tiger who had recently left the company of his mother to lead an independent existence. He established his headquarters near Thola Kot, around 8 km from Tamli in Champawat District. He lived on pigs, jaraos (a hill name for sambhar), kakkars and ghorals. He showed his presence by occasionally emitting deep growls but never harmed the cattle of that area. So I christened him 'The Bachelor of Thola Kot'. I saw the Bachelor for the first time when he suddenly came out of the deep ravine and crossed the forest road. I and Dhani Ram, a retired forest guard and an old friend of mine, saw him with amusement and curiosity.

Thola Kot village in Champawat district

During my next visit to Tamli, Dhani Ram came all the way from his village to meet me. The old man had plenty of time on his hands, and after dwelling at length on his family, and smoking *bidis*, he turned the conversation on the Bachelor who, as he said, had killed a number of village cattle, which was both unusual and distressing as it caused a big loss to the village folk. I was on my holidays and I expressed my wish to go to Thola Kot to which Dhani Ram readily agreed. The following morning when the day was young, we five set out for Thola Kot with Dhani Ram in the lead. On our way, my poor but loving companions could not make out my Christian name and addressed me as

"Jail *Shaab*" with a smile on their faces. Our way lay through rugged terrain and the path was slippery because it had rained the previous night. The entire valley was shrouded in mist. My other four companions were as surefooted as a mountain goat.

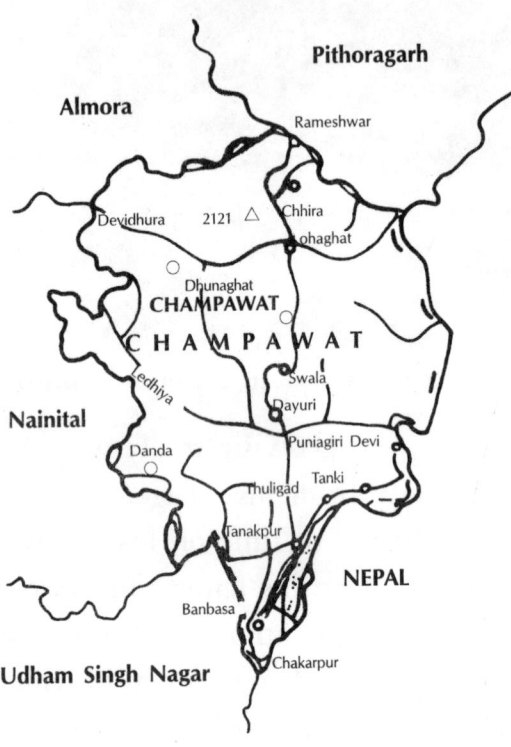

I, on the other hand, was slightly inexperienced and often lagged behind them. After slipping on the ground and stumbling over the rocks a number of times, we reached a ravine. Here, Dhani Ram stopped and told me we had arrived in the Bachelor's territory and asked us to move cautiously. As chance would have it, we had hardly gone for some distance when we heard a deep growl followed by a low muttering sound. This was unusual. We thought it prudent not to move forward and retraced our steps. After a short while we again heard two sounds simultaneously. Leaving the men to the safety of a knoll, I and Dhani Ram climbed up a rock to have a look into the ravine. Slowly we raised our heads and saw two tigers. The Bachelor was frolicking and flirting with a tigress. When the game was over the tigers entered the ravine. On our way to the village, we advised the villagers not to send their cattle in that area.

I hope the Bachelor survived and did not fall to the bullets of greedy poachers and that he fathered some healthy offspring.

❑❑❑

4

The Drongo's Perfect Signal

Jim Corbett, while writing about the man-eater of Panar, has given a fascinating account of two drongos showing their reliability. The sun was setting behind the hills of Sanouli village in Pithoragarh district. The inhabitants of the village were terror-stricken. Corbett was sitting on an old, stunted oak tree awaiting the arrival of the man-eater which had killed about 400 human beings in the area. Suddenly, two drongos, which were also sitting on the top branch of the same tree, flew off and began to bait some animal. The birds gave the perfect signal to Corbett about the approach of the man-eater near the tree, which Corbett killed. Martin Booth, the biographer of Jim Corbett, has also made a passing reference of these two birds in his book.

Like the babbler, shrike and thrush, the drongo is one of the most reliable guards in the forest. It warns the jungle folk about the presence of some carnivore, snake or mongoose in the vicinity. Whenever the bird sees them, it begins to hover over them and when the occasion arises, it strikes them with its sharp beak.

It is agile, slim and black in colour and its tail is long and forked. There are seven species of this bird found in the Indian sub-continent. The bird can be seen perched on wires, telegraph lines or on some old stunted tree. The bird moves about in the company of the mynah, egret, heron, roller and starling. It is fond of riding on the back of domestic cattle. It is an early riser and makes the *'chenchoo chenchoo'* call.

The drongo eats grasshoppers, insects and caterpillars. The bird is very useful for farmers, as it eats various insects which are harmful for the crop. It also eats ticks from the bodies of the animals. When there is a little fire in the grass or jungle, one can see these birds chasing away insects and grasshoppers and eating them.

These birds build their nest on the high branches of the tree and guard it defiantly. Their main enemies are hawks and falcons.

Once, while roaming about the forest, I saw these two birds perched on the top branch of a tree, guarding their nest. Suddenly, one of these two birds flew off and began to chase a crow. In the meanwhile, a falcon also joined in the race and flew after the drongo and caught it from behind.

The poor drongo struggled for some time but the falcon did not relinquish its hold and disappeared among the trees with the bird.

The laws of the jungle are harsh and hard.

Danger and uncertainty loom large and only those who are fit and strong can survive and rule.

5

Chuka: The Tigers' Heartland

In today's cyberage when some self-styled champions of wildlife are using it not only for prompt publicity but also to make quick money, do we ever care to know about Chuka, once the heartland of tigers? It was in the vicinity of Chuka that four man-eaters—Talla Des, Thak, Chuka and one more—were shot. It is these tigers that are the main characters of Jim Corbett's works that generated tremendous interest about tigers in the hearts of millions of people all over the world. So Chuka was my destination.

Chuka, as the local legend goes, means missing. It is on the confluence point of the Ladhya and the Sarda rivers, and the last village on India's border, for across the Sarda is Nepal. On three sides it is surrounded by the Sarda at an altitude of around

4,000 feet, and probably is an entry point of tigers into India.

Chuka village near which the man-eaters of Chuka and Thak were killed

A small goat track runs from Thulighat. On the left flank are the tall ridges many hundred feet high, atop one of which is the temple of Purnagiri, and down below flows the Sarda in her pristine purity. The falling of rocks is a common phenomenon, and one false step will hurl one in the deep swirling water of the Sarda. If J C Pandey, a police-superintendent and my friend, reads these lines, he should know how useful he proved in my one-man mission to Chuka. To reach Chuka is a hazardous task, if not impossible.

The red glow of the setting sun was fading off the Nepal hills when I reached this remote village.

The watchman and the forest guard of Kaladhunga (not Kaladhungi) forest bungalow (about which I will tell on some other occasion) had been told about my visit, and they made some arrangements for my three-day stay in the village itself.

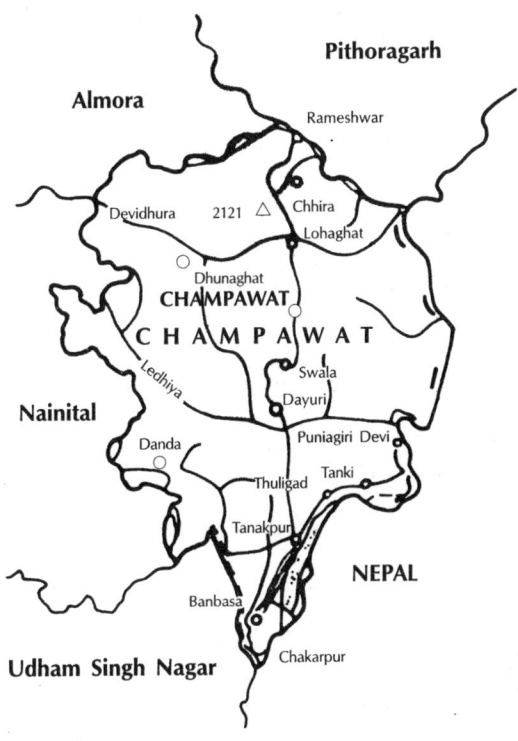

The news on my arrival caught like a wildfire in the village, and the words 'some *sahib* has come to visit us' came from their mouths. People in this part of our country are very poor, gullible and a little superstitious. Motorable road is around 25 km from here; people have to walk down to purchase provisions for their home and carry them back on their head; and a cup of tea and a tablet of Disprin are still precious commodities.

The next day I went to the confluence point of the Ladhya and the Sarda where I saw the fresh pug marks of a tiger which the previous night had crossed over to the Chuka side from Sem village. Sem is sandwiched between the Ladhya and the Sarda and even today remains cut off from the rest of the country for at least three months during the rainy season. "We have to procure ration and other provisions for our families for three months, for the Ladhya and the Sarda are in spate," said Ashok Singh of Sem village. I went along the steep bank of the Ladhya and reached the stream near which once grew a ficus tree from which the Chuka man-eater was shot. Regrettably, I could not find the tree as I was alone and it was getting dark.

One evening Umed Singh, an elderly man of 66, came to meet me. He showed me the *bail* tree near which the officials' camp used to be pitched during their different visits to Chuka.

Fortunately, this tree and the ground have not been ravaged by the twists and turns of time and bear a silent testimony to many an unknown brave Indian who lived in Chuka, which has been immortalised by Jim Corbett in his works, if not by us.

❏❏❏

6

Poacher's Delight

The Terai region of Uttar Pradesh, stretching from the Himalayan foothills near Bijnor to the borders of Nepal, is nearly always lush, and abounds in romantic stories of tigers and *shikar*. In the 50s, the region was an inviting strip of heaven, peerless in its exotic wildlife and dense sal forests, celebrated by Jim Corbett in his five-volume tribute to the land and life of India.

My father, a post-master in a small town in the Terai, and in the style of the Raj days, was not only a good shot but also a good sport with a large circle of friends. They would throng our house every morning and evening, for a round of *gup-shup* and tea. One day, my father introduced to our house a new friend, Gardner *Sahib*—a sprightly man in his late 40s, whose silver brows and crown contrasted sharply with his dark face. Gardner *Sahib* had an unusually large family, going even by the sizes of those days, the crane dropping a baby down the chimney of his house every year.

He locomoted about the town on a rickety bicycle, and always carried a catapult in his hip-pocket. His catapult, he often claimed, was so powerful and accurate that using it, he had once caused three highwaymen to flee after they had confronted him in the forest. We, the town's youngsters, never could check the veracity of his claims, but were generally in awe of the man and not entirely for reasons—of his prowess with the catapult.

Gardner *Sahib* was an admirer of beauty, and this he made plain as daylight by frequenting Paaroo, the comely widow who lived by the edge of the town with her two young sons. Gradually, Gardner *Sahib* became quite friendly with them too, and forged an alliance with Paaroo's elder son, Chhaatoo. The two would often slip deep into the forest by night, and come up with their trophies, or timber, to make a tidy sum from their adventure, much to the persistent annoyance of the forest department.

Years later, as young collegiates at Lucknow, a bunch of us one summer evening visited Gardner

Sahib at his pressing invitation to see some wildlife. Our excitement ran high as we set out on our bicycles at the crack of the dawn the next day. As we meandered our way along the dust track, growing heat and humidity of the day slowed down our progress. Despite hours of labour, we seemed nowhere near the elusive forest or the exotic fowl and meal on hoof that abounded in it. Rather reluctantly we decided to call off the expedition, and our host graciously asked us to return home and await him.

This man of the wilds, of foibles and peccadilloes, warm heart and lively humour, surfaced early next morning, with a beaming face. And immediately set about transforming some of the wildlife specimens we had missed seeing into delicious *kababs* and *biryani*. The memory of that 'wild' feast came rolling down to me recently when on a recent visit to an obscure village near Bijnor, I stood before his humble lasting abode marked by a moss-covered tombstone.

❏❏❏

7

Kaladhunga Forest Bungalow

Undoubtedly, the Britishers were not only great lovers of wildlife but also committed to its protection and preservation. They made a number of strict forest laws, and forest bungalows which their forest officials visited with regularity and a sense of commitment. One of the most beautiful forest bungalows I have ever seen in my life was the Kaladhunga forest bungalow. This, however, should not be mistaken for Kaladhungi bungalow, now a national museum.

Many years ago there lived a man, named Kalu, and he had a *dunga* (boat). So the word 'Kaladhunga', as the locals say, has been derived from these words. This beautiful bungalow is situated in the cone-shaped peninsula, which is around six kilometres long and two kilometres wide. It is situated on the bank of the Sarda river which forms a boundary between India and Nepal. When the sun rises early in the morning over the Nepal hills, one can have a panoramic and unforgettable view of the mighty Himalayas which once formed an impenetrable barrier between India and its neighbours. Come night, and one can hear the call of kakkar, ghoral, sambhar, bear, leopard and sometimes tiger.

Kaladhunga forest bungalow

The evening was drawing in when I reached this bungalow, much to the relief of the forest *chowkidar* who had been informed about my visit. He showed me the three-roomed building which had been made almost a hundred years ago. It has a kitchen, a toilet, and a sprawling lawn where, it is said, the British officers played tennis. Scores of celebrated British officials, such as Lord Hailey, McDonald of forest department, Sir Ibbotson, deputy commissioner of Kumaon, his wife Jean Ibbotson visited and lived in this bungalow. All around the bungalow once there grew a beautiful garden. Alas! much to my dismay and disappointment, I saw wild grass growing in abundance with no provision to mow it even once in a year. "Do you not mow the wild grass?" I asked Kashi Ram, the *chowkidar*.

"I have no implement to cut it," he replied firmly.

With the passage of time, this beautiful building has developed cracks, and a little cement has been applied to cover the cracks, but no efforts have been made to repair the yawning cracks, which clearly indicates our casual and cavalier approach for the protection of this monument. The building leaks badly in the rainy season.

It is made of stone-brick and sal wood has been used for the ceiling, windows and doors. Fortunately, the sal wood is still intact, and the varnish and paint, which had been used in the earlier times, has withstood the onslaught of time.

There are two other buildings close to it. One, as the plate shows, was built in 1920 as a forest post and the other, for servants. The forest post is unoccupied, in a crumbling state and may fall any day.

In the absence of ration supply, I decided to move to Chuka. It was getting dark and I was going along the goat-track followed by the *chowkidar* a few metres behind. While going round a bend, I bumped into a black bear and a short two-cornered race that followed between me and the bear. I beat him by a comfortable margin much to the joy of only one spectator—the *chowkidar* who was shouting vociferously *'shabash, shabash'*. Such small and harmless encounters between a man and a beast makes our life so thrilling.

Generations have gone and will go, but the Kaladhunga forest bungalow will remain a mute witness as to how committed and honest we are for the preservation of our forests and such beautiful monuments, now a part of our wildlife heritage.

❑❑❑

8

A Visit to **Sanouli**

On a blasting cold day of January, I set off on a jeep from Lohaghat with my camera accompanied by a guide which my host had provided to me. My guide was one of the most interesting jungle characters I have ever met. He was short in stature, as round as a football and had a pair of eyes which were so small that I could hardly make out whether he was awake or asleep. Ahead of Dhunaghat I part with my readers, for some of you may go to the age-old shrine of Dabidhura for *darshan* while I take the other road, for my destination lies far ahead in the north. We left the jeep and set out on our arduous journey. Up and down we went through treacherous terrain where even one false step could have resulted in multiple fractures or even very unpleasant death.

I myself visualised hundreds of man-eaters stalking me from bushes and sometimes regretted my self-imposed task. My guide, who up to that moment had remained silent, suddenly said, "*Shaab, mera photo khincho*" and I duly obliged him.

After a little distance again he said, "*Shaab phir se khincho*". This was too much. To lose one's temper in the forest is of no consequence. However, to keep him in good humour, I offered him *bidis* which he smoked with great relish.

When we nearly reached the Panar river, my guide asked me, "Why are you going to Sanouli village?" I said, "To know about the man-eating *bagh* (leopard)." This was the beginning of further trouble. He immediately reversed his position and asked me to walk in front while he bore the rear. The word 'man-eater' creates an inferiority complex in oneself and my guide was no exception.

To cross the Panar river was a problem, as the water was ice-cold and the stones slippery. I was as much worried about the safety of my limbs as about my camera. Having crossed the river, the guide climbed a commanding point and shouted some message to three women carrying bundles of sticks on their head. The only word I could make out was Sanouli. When the sun was a hand's breadth from the snow-capped mountains, we reached Sanouli. There I saw some people whose relatives had been killed by the man-eater, the thicket which the man-eater had used as its hideout and the place where it had been killed.

Both man-eater and the legendary *shikari*, Carpet *Sahib*, have gone to meet their Maker but have enabled me to tell you this narrative.

❏❏❏

9

The Temple and the Tiger

It was the month of April when the legendary Jim Corbett reached Dabidhura in pursuit of the Panar man-eater which had claimed more than 400 human lives in that area and about which I will tell you on some other occasion. The road was very steep and Jim reached the Rest House weary and tired. He consumed tea and feasted his eyes on the breathtaking view of the valley. It was evening when the old *pundit* of Dabidhura temple, with whom Jim had made friends while shooting the Champawat man-eater, came to see him. Both Jim and the *pundit* sat late into the evening chatting and smoking cigarettes. At the end of the conversation Jim asked the *pundit* if he could have some shooting in the area. The *pundit* replied: "Yes there is the temple tiger. I have no objection, *sahib*, to your trying to shoot the tiger, but neither you nor anyone else will ever succeed in killing it." Finally, it was the *pundit* that proved correct. In five days Jim saw the tiger eight times and pressed the trigger four times but the bullets could not even graze the tiger. It was only to verify the facts that recently I went on my mission to Dabidhura.

The old temple of Dabidhura

It was 8.30 p.m. when I reached the small town of Lohaghat which was shrouded in mist and there was no place for me to stay. Soon Kirti Chand Murari, a young lad of a respectable family stepped out of a jeep and took me to his house and made me comfortable. Reposing faith in some unknown man is possible only in India and nowhere else in the world. The following day, the lad offered his services to take me to Dabidhura which is around 45 km from Lohaghat.

On reaching Dabidhura, I took the road that leads to the temple. In place of the old temple I found a new temple, but the back portion of the temple and the steps are still intact. Soon the new young *pundit* came to meet me. He took me inside the temple and showed me the *chabutra* where a herdsman had once been attacked by the Panar man-eater.

The young *pundit* sat by my side and told me many stories about the temple. At last I asked him,

"Is the Temple Tiger a reality?" At this he replied: "*Sahib*, you see the entire area is surrounded by dense forest, and the tiger often makes his appearance here." "But what is the mystery about the tiger of this area?" I further inquired of him. To prove his point, he told me that *ashthbali* is performed here from May to August and no one can even touch the bones of the animal. According to him, once a man came here to collect the the bones of the sacrificed animal and the tiger appeared in the vicinity of the temple. The man atoned for his mistake and dropped the bones at the right place.

The old temple and the tiger have withered away with the passage of time leaving their indelible print on the tablet of my memory.

❑❑❑

10

A Night of Terror

In between Lohaghat and Dabidhura is the small village of Dhunaghat. It is a forked road—one road goes to Dabidhura, known all over India for its old temple, and one newly constructed road links it with Almora. It was my first visit to this area, and I was staying with Bhisht*ji* who knew every inch of the forest of this area. During the British Raj, many British engineers and forest officials had stayed in his house.

After two days, he expressed his desire to accompany me to Dabidhura to fetch his daughter who had been living there and nursing a child. We reached Dabidhura around noon. While Bhisht*ji* went to meet his relations, I set off in the west of Dabidhura along with an old man who had come running from his house to meet me. "Panar man-eater and the Temple tiger?" he asked me. "How do you know this?" I retorted. "*Sahib*, my grandfather had seen the bear when it had been shot, and he also received the fat of the animal." He gladly took me for around three kilometres to the west to show the place near which the epic fight between the tiger and the bear took place.

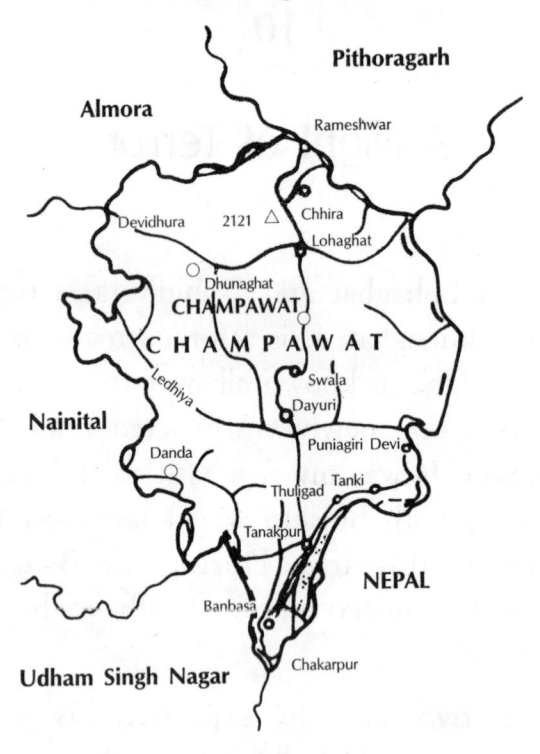

[Map showing region with locations: Pithoragarh, Almora, Rameshwar, Devidhura, 2121, Chhira, Lohaghat, Dhunaghat, CHAMPAWAT, Ledhiya, Swala, Dayuri, Nainital, Danda, Puniagiri Devi, Thuligad, Tanki, Tanakpur, Banbasa, NEPAL, Udham Singh Nagar, Chakarpur]

At sundown I returned to Dabidhura and was joined by Bhisht*ji* and his daughter. We hired a jeep for Dhunaghat. Call it *kismat*, luck or destiny, it sometimes plays scurvy tricks with our life. We had hardly gone for five kilometres when the jeep broke down necessitating a forced march of 10 kilometres. We had gone a short distance when a barking deer began to bark hysterically behind us. I was armed only with a two-cell torch. As I switched on the torch, I saw a big leopard. It lay flat on the ground. Leopards were a common sight in those days in this part of the country, so we continued our journey. After two hundred metres I again switched on the torch, and saw the leopard following close behind us. However, this time it began to twitch its tail and growl. This was the eventuality for which I was least prepared. At night, a human being is the most helpless thing in the world. I was more concerned with the safety of the young mother and her child. So we began to move in a bunch and talk loudly, for this was the only means of defence we had.

As luck would have it, we saw a man returning late from his field shouldering a yoke and followed by two bullocks. In a jungle, strength lies in number, so the leopard had no chance save to leave the field. And we all heaved a sigh of relief. On reaching Dhunaghat, the brave girl set about preparing tea and food for us without any fuss.

After many years, when I reflect upon the incident, I feel chilled with fear. But my heart goes out to the brave young mother whose only answer to my question was: "Facing danger makes one morally strong."   ❑❑❑

11

The Man who Fought a Tigress

Many of you might have read the stories of Greek heroes like Hercules and Atlas, knowing fully well that these are based on mythology. India is a country of the brave who have done many great deeds which have sadly gone unnoticed. Many heroes have died unhonoured in their own land and in their own country.

My father, who was on the staff of the viceroy and a crack shot, initiated me into jungle craft in my childhood. Ever since, love for the jungles has become a part of my life and my objective was to know the name of that powerful man who had hurled a man-eating tigress who had killed 64 human beings around Dalkania village in Nainital. A discovery, however small it may be, gives an immense sense of satisfaction. When I succeeded in discovering the name of this man for the first time after having made some painstaking efforts, my joy knew no bounds. This man was none other than Kulumani, probably one of the most powerfully built and the bravest man India has ever produced. On knowing where he lived, my destination became Dalkania.

Keshav Dutt Bhat whose grandmother, Nirla Devi, was attacked by the Chowgarh man-eater and treated by Jim Corbett

I reached Khansui by jeep and from there, I had to go on foot for 25 kilometres, and reached Dalkania absolutely bone tired and hungry. Here a *bania* placed a room at my disposal. Soon people in twos and threes began to pour into the room and in a while, the room was flocked with people of different sizes and shapes, looking at me with surprise, for I was the first person who had ever gone there to write about the brave Kulumani. Finally, Keshav Dutt Bhat offered to tell me about the hero.

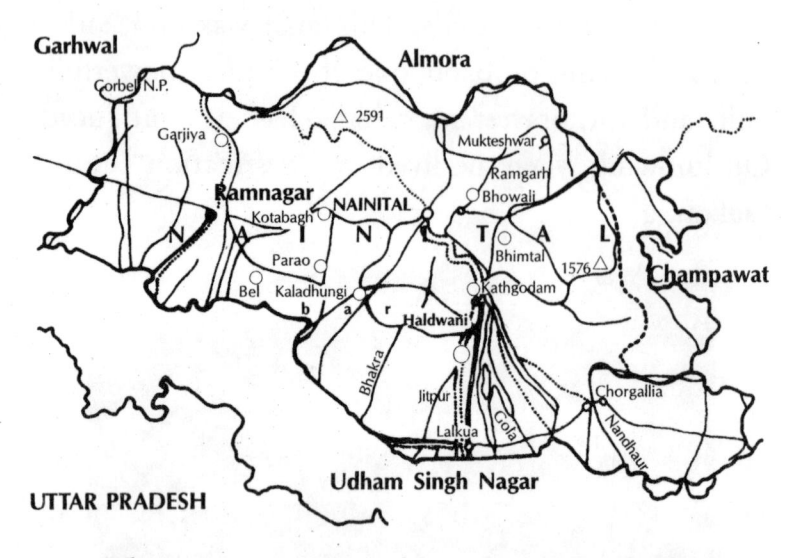

The next morning, this man came all the way to show me the place where that epic fight had taken place. In the north of Dalkania and four kilometres away is the Nandhor river. Up and down and down and up we went through rugged terrain. The Nandhor valley is comparatively plain. After crossing the river, we went up the steep hill through a goat track. Here we turned to the left and finally reached a place from where we could see the white rock.

"You know *sahib*, Kulumani was cutting the grass here with his son when the tigress attacked him. Kulumani fell on his back while the tigress lay on him—chest to chest. Very slowly he brought his legs against her belly. Then he lifted the tigress with all his strength and hurled her from the mountain." "Was he so powerful and strong?" I asked him. "Yes sir, he was the most powerful man in all the adjoining villages, and we were afraid of him. He was very talkative and also kind-hearted."

The red glow of the setting sun was dying off the hills when we reached Adhoura village. The village folks were very hospitable and soon made arrangements for our night stay. Here, people told me of many heroic deeds of the people of the village. They told me how a young boy fought with an adult leopard who had attacked him in the house, for more than half an hour.

Next day at the crack of dawn, I set off for Dalkania, but my progress was delayed because of a pair of leopards I found basking on the goat track. I reached Dalkania in the evening and soon went to sleep, forgetting of tigers and leopards.

Hundreds of heroes had come and will come, but can anyone match the brave deeds of this simple and illiterate son of India? Never!

12

My Friend Goonga

He was a skinny and loose limbed stripling with a lean and hungry face. As he was deaf and dumb since birth, we called him 'Goonga'. I spotted him for the first time at a party in my cousin's house at Moradabad and took him to be an urchin. As I grew familiar with him, I was forced to change my opinion and found him to be one of the bravest handicapped gentlemen I have ever known.

Goonga lived at Harthala near Moradabad and belonged to the *Bhantu* tribe. Our house was on the fringe of a forest and to protect the life of our young ones, poultry and cattle, we hired the services of Goonga who discharged his duties with scrupulous honesty. His ancestor, Sultana, the undisputed bandit king in India during the 1920s, had established a reign of terror in the erstwhile United Provinces and Punjab.

My cousins and I used to indulge in target shooting with a Diana air gun as a pastime. In this game too, Goonga beat us four square, always hitting the bull's eye. His knowledge of jungle craft was flawless and he was familiar with every inch of the forest in our area and knew where game could be had. Whenever we went out for partridge shooting, it was Goonga's duty to arrange the beat. If he had located any partridge or jungle fowl, he would clap his hands to indicate the direction of the flying bird to the gunner. At the end of the shoot it was Goonga's job to give the *shikaris* their share. On our way back home, he would lead the party, displaying our trophies to passers-by and friends.

One winter day, our elders sent Goonga and me to collect some payment from a village. I had heard reports about a pack of wolves operating in that area. Dusk was setting in. As we reached the outskirts of the village, some agitated voices followed by the wailing of women could be heard. I alerted Goonga. The next moment we saw a wolf holding a child by the waist and running in our direction. The sight spurred Goonga to chase the wolf. Sensing danger, the wolf dropped the child and fled into the nearby bushes. The villagers who had now converged on the spot, were all praise for Goonga, for saving a human life literally from the jaws of death. The child is now a full-grown man but still bears teeth marks on his back.

Several years after the chilling incident, I visited my cousin's house again. A party was in full swing but something was amiss. Later on, my cousin told me of the sudden demise of Goonga when he was barely on the threshold of life.

There are some special moments in life which neither time nor tide can ever erase from memory. The beautiful moments I shared in the forest in the company of this man who showed exemplary courage despite his handicap are indelible; they are a part of my treasured memories.

❑❑❑

13

The Brave Widow of **Thak**

On November 18, 2000, I became the first Indian writer to have reached the village of Thak to write about Naraini, a brave widow who is living alone with her three small children in this deserted village surrounded by very dense forest with no human habitation for miles around, where one can see poisonous snakes, leopards, marauding bears and sometimes tigers, even during the day time, moving around her house.

Though many of us might have read about the brave deeds done by some women of the world, but the story of this brave woman has few parallels in the history of the world. It was my friend, Mathura Dutt Pandey, one of the chief *purohits* of Purnagiri temple, who inspired me to go at least once to this village and see how brave Indian women are.

As I was photographing the rock from where the Thak man-eater was shot, I saw a woman toiling up the mountain carrying some provisions on her back followed by her small son. As she drew near, she stopped and asked me if I am the *sahib* who has come from Delhi to write about Thak. On my confirming that I was the same man, she smiled feebly.

Naraini with her son Govind in Thak forest

"How long have you been living here?" I asked. "I came here right after my marriage. But one day my husband Shishu Pal Singh died. My small children went to Chuka village and six people came to cremate my husband," she replied.

"Have you any relations?"

"Yes *sahib*, but they are living far away from this village; though the message was sent about my husband's death, nobody came to share my sorrow; all left me alone. Sometimes an *angrez sahib* comes here in this forest, but you are the only Indian writer who has come to see me."

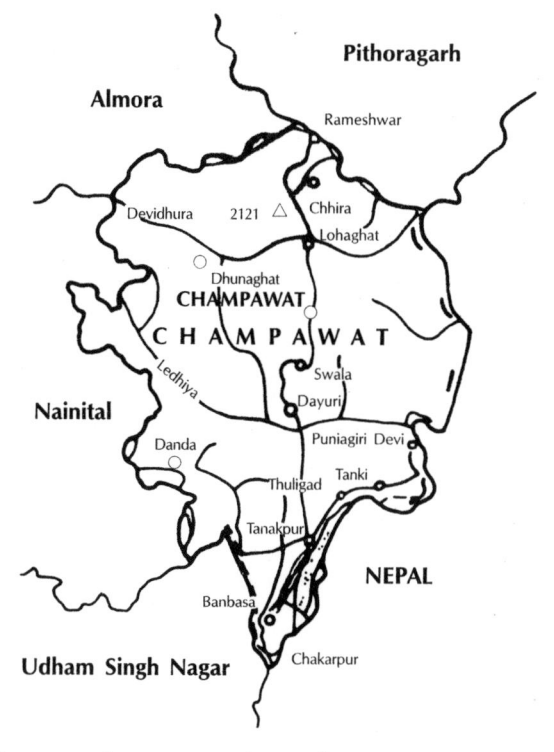

"How do you subsist?"

"I have a small holding, and the land is poor. I till the land myself with the help of my three children. I have a few head of cattle, but in the hills cattle give little milk. Whatever we grow, we subsist on it. Help of any kind is impossible."

"Are you not afraid of the wild animals?"

"There are a number of dangerous wild animals, such as leopards, bears and tigers. One can see them moving about the area even during the daytime. During heavy rains and intense cold, some of these animals come and take shelter in the deserted houses once occupied by the *pundits* who have all left this village now. A number of times they have harmed my cattle. But my children, though small, are the bravest children in this area. They know how to face even a tiger. But who bothers about the bravery and hardship of the poor."

At the end I put a little money in the palm of her son for I am a man of meagre resources, which the boy accepted with a sense of gratitude. She very honestly asked me if I could take any of her sons so that he could earn his living by honest means and hard work. I found myself a wretched impostor in her presence.

The cycle of life and nature never ends. For us, Naraini's life of sorrow, suffering and hardship will always remain a source of inspiration for today, tomorrow and evermore.

❏❏❏

14

Tryst with a Tigress

David Morrison's burning ambition was to 'shoot' a tiger. A dashing, young adventurous Scotsman, David was a wildlife photographer of some repute. His love for the wilds had taken him to far corners of the world, from Australia's great outbacks to the dense jungles of Kenya, and from Canada's birch forests to South Africa's safari lands. Though he had shot many wild species with his camera, Stripes had eluded him.

Discussing his obsession with his relatives in Scotland one day, he got a tip. One of his relations mentioned my father with whom he had worked at the Viceroy's camp at Dehra Dun during World War II. After an exchange of letters, David turned up at our house in a sleepy town in the Terai one mid-December day. As my father was unwell, the task of escorting David to our friend's farm close to the Corbett National Park fell upon me.

Assured by villagers that there was no man-eater or rogue elephant in the vicinity, we set up camp and set out into the jungle. For three days we spotted kakkar, cheetal, sambhar, hog deer, red jungle fowl, black partridge and pheasant, and even saw a tiger's pugmarks. But the tiger remained elusive.

On the fourth day, an early morning visit from two forest officials and a chat with them over a hot cup of tea saw us trudging our way through the thick foliage to a well-covered *machan* they had made for themselves a few days ago. Here they helped us clamber up, and left after giving us some useful tips.

We had been on the *machan* for barely 20-25 minutes when we heard a low growl. We moved our heads in that direction, and from the corner of my eye I saw David pick up his camera. Presently, a fullgrown tigress in the prime of her youth, her coat shining, came into view with two cubs in tow. Instead of moving on, as we expected, she lay down on the ground close to the *machan*, and pointedly raised her nose in our direction. She was suspicious of our presence, of this I was quite sure.

Whenever the gambolling cubs moved towards our tree, she would emit a low growl and the cubs would retrace their steps back to her.

After basking in the sun for quite a while, she slipped behind the thick bushes followed by the cubs, and vanished from sight. A cheetal's alarm call some distance away told us that she had withdrawn deep into the jungle. Quickly but silently, we climbed down the tree and hurried back to our camp. Packing up, we made for home, the happiest men on earth.

That night David developed the rolls of films he had shot, and made prints. Christmas eve next day saw the collected family and friends eagerly poring over the pictures, featuring the proud mother and her energetic cubs. It was David's day all right. Besides accolades for his photographs, he also won the jackpot of Rs 101 for singing the best carol of the evening—"Silent night, Holy night..."

❑❑❑

15

Old Man and the Forest

"We should save our ecology and wildlife, else we too will perish one day," were the sane words of Munshi Ram, a patriarch of Katkanoula village.

As I was discussing wildlife over a cup of tea with a forest official in a restaurant at Ramnagar, he suggested my going to Munshi Ram's village and getting in touch with him. The following day, travelling via Garjia and Mohan, I reached his village in the evening. The whole countryside is rugged and is cut up by deep ravines and rock cliffs, sometimes many hundred metres deep. Over this area, villages of varying sizes are scattered. Once it was the domain of the Mohan man-eater.

Luck plays an important part in one's life and I was lucky to have met this old man as he was about to leave the village. He is coffee-coloured and of frail frame. He wears a *khadi* kurta, pyjama and a Gandhi cap. He is more than 80 years old.

Munshi Ram of Katkanoula village

The hill commanded an extensive view of the terrain which was covered by lush green forests. "These forests come under *gram panchayats* of respective villages. Our life depends to a great extent on these forests," remarked Munshi Ram. The forests, undoubtedly, show the eco-consciousness of the people of this area. If there is any forest fire or any epidemic, it is the villagers who first take some remedial steps.

Munshi Ram has hardly used any medicine in his life. "Whenever I fall sick, I take some herbs and get all right," he remarked. People of this area are quite poor but sturdy and strong. I have not seen any MBBS doctor for miles around. "There is an abundant growth of medicinal plants in this area but not much research has been done, and only a few such as *panja, garur panja, sameo, atish, gokul, masi, adjari* and *tetra* are being used in medicine," he lamented.

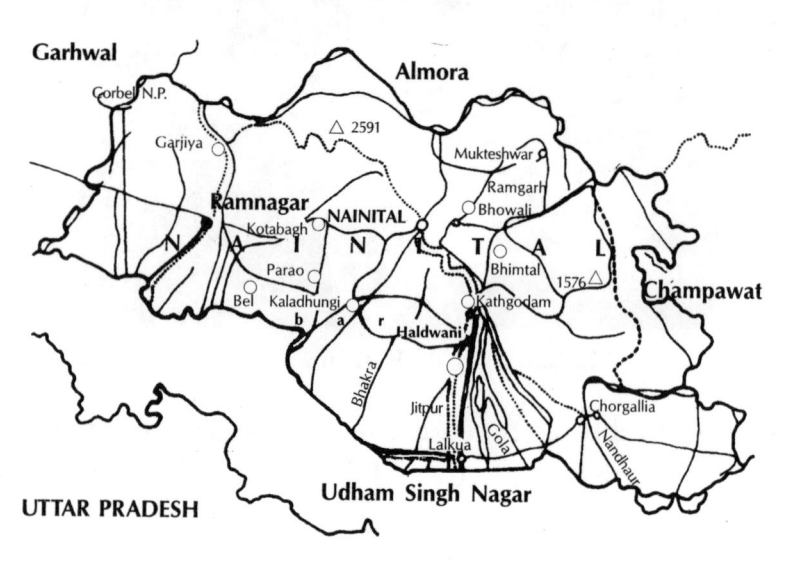

He is a great lover of wildlife. According to him, wild animals and birds form an important component of ecology and show the health of the forest. Animals like kakkars, ghorals and sambhars move about freely in this area and enjoy full protection of the people. He told me he had seen the Mohan man-eater when it had been killed.

With Mohan behind me, I reached Garjia. The temple of Garjia is situated on a small hillock and is surrounded by the water of the Kosi river. It is Garjia as some believe which protects the life of the denizens of forest and human beings of this area. As the shadows lengthened, I decided to depart for my way lay far in the east.

As I am writing this account, the words of Munshi Ram are still ringing in my ears: "I love my forests and nature, for nature manifests God. One day my ashes will mingle with nature."

❑❑❑

16

On a Man-eater's Trail

The scenic town of Champawat, now a district headquarter in Kumaon, is synonymous with a man-eating tigress which had once killed more than 434 human beings before it fell to the bullets of Corbett. My plan was to track the jungle from where the man-eater had operated.

That year, in the middle of July, I reached Champawat. It was raining heavily when I reached Phoolbari. My host, Rev. Abert Singh, put one room at my disposal and explained me the route to Chawra village.

The following day, taking good wishes of my host and others I set out on my mission. I took the Lohaghat Road and on reaching Sonjh village, I left the road and turned to the left. From here, the jungle starts which is not so dense as it was because of persistent pressure of human population. It consists mainly of pine and deodar trees. The land is comparatively plain. On reaching the power house, I climbed a steep hill and reached the crest of the hill, almost in a bath of sweat. Beyond it lay terraced fields of some acres and the Chawra village.

My approach was observed by the villagers who began to come in twos and threes and soon a small crowd gathered around me. I had scarcely taken my seat when a steaming cup of tea was placed in my hand. An 80-year old man, Khem Singh, sat at my feet and gave a thrilling account how the man-eater was killed as his father had a grandstand view of the entire proceedings. "You see these hills across the gorge; the beat started from there on the order of Carpit *Sahib* and *tehsildar*. Many people of our village such as Karam Singh, Harak Singh, Chandra Singh, Gopal Singh and Shoban Singh took part in the beat. People of other villages such as Phoonjar, Chawki, Simalta, Kathar, Pali and Chanawla also took part in the beat." At 2 p.m. I returned to the small power house to have lunch with Gopal Singh, the *pradhan* of Chawra village. After finishing our food, we set out in the southwest direction. After climbing many boulders and rocks, we reached a big rock. Here Gopal Singh stopped and pointed his finger towards the gorge and said, "This is the place where the man-eater had been killed and you are among the few brave and fortunate, including some foreigners, who have come all the way from Champawat on foot to see it. The place is sacred to us and a part of our heritage."

Now evening was advancing and I had a difficult and long way to go, so I decided to make for Champawat. On my way back I saw a number of small children returning from school, absolutely oblivious that once a dreaded man-eater traversed the same ground and struck terror in the hearts of their forefathers.

❑❑❑

17

Mysterious Forest Lights

Some years ago, a parley took place between former US president Ronald Reagan and the Russian president Gorbachev in Reykjyavik, Iceland, in a haunted house. And few years back, a TV channel telecast a programme, probably titled 'Things Extraordinary', showing some mysterious objects, apparitions and voices operating in very strange ways in different parts of the world, such as USA, Australia and Great Britain. The telecast showed how the paintings of a painter were spoilt of their own, how a shadow followed a woman, and how mysterious voices and shadows appeared at the dead of night in the deserted jails of Tasmania. This clearly shows that some mysterious powers and forces work in our universe which human mind can never interpret, for human mind is limited.

Similarly, some strange lights appear in the forest near the temple of Purnagiri, probably one of the most sacred and famous temples of Uttaranchal, some kilometres away from the town of Tanakpur. Here, people from all walks of life flock to pay respect to the goddess Bhagvati. Down

Temple of Purnagiri across which the lights appear

below flows the Sarda river in its pristine purity. This river serves as a natural boundary between Nepal and India. Since Thak village has become deserted now, some of the *pundits* have changed their headquarters to Purnagiri. One day, I reached this shrine on the invitation of my old friend *pundit* Mathura Dutt Pandey who now is one of the chief *purohits* of this temple.

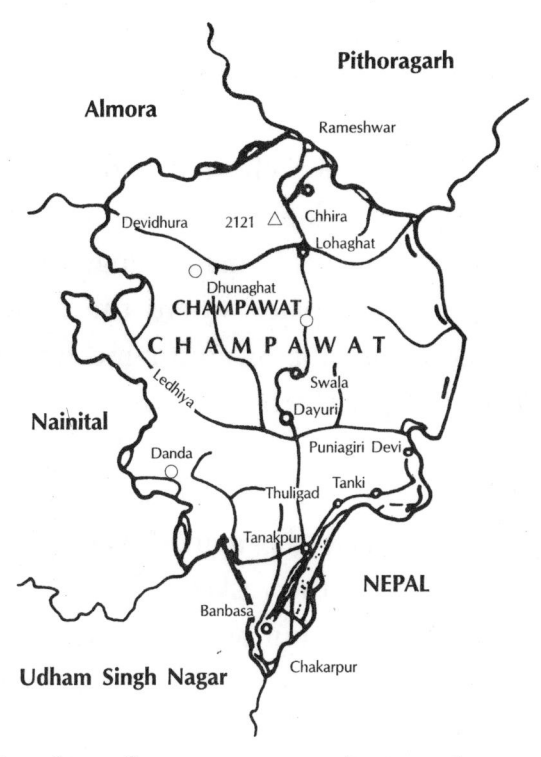

In the afternoon, *punditji* took me up the summit where the temple exists. On the way, we discussed about the question of life and death and many issues which are still beyond the ken of human knowledge. On reaching the summit, I asked *punditji* about the mysterious lights about which I had read and heard a good deal earlier. He remarked that he had also heard about these lights which appear across the Sarda on the side of Nepal. Later on, he took me to the other side of the peak and showed the place where the mysterious lights are believed to appear some times.

On my next visit to Chuka, I passed through that rugged terrain strewn with big boulders and surrounded by thick forest which once was the heartland of tigers, especially man-eating tigers. As I neared the place, I looked across the river and saw smooth rocks where human beings can't get a foothold. It was that place where the mysterious lights are believed to appear. With me was a man of Tatta Pani village which was across the river in the Nepal side. "How many times have you seen the lights?" I inquired of him. "I saw the lights on two occasions," replied the man. "Were you alone and frightened?" I further asked. "I was travelling with four other people, but as we saw the lights on the rocks, we were extremely frightened," he remarked.

On my way back from Chuka, I was accompanied by Tirlochan Bhatt, a forest guard. I also asked him the same question to which he candidly replied: "One evening I was going with an *angrez sahib,* and it got dark so we slept in a cave. Round about midnight, we heard the wailing of some women near our cave. When we switched on our torch, we saw nothing except darkness all around us. Deep in the jungles many mysterious things happen of which this materialistic world can never know," he replied.

These mysterious forest lights are an established fact, but I can't advance an explanation to that effect. They will always remain shrouded in mystery.

❏❏❏

18

Bachelor Boy

Some bachelors are eccentric, and this is the price they pay for being bachelors. My friend, Cutlar, was one of the most eligible and well-established bachelors I have had the pleasure to meet. To prove his bachelor status, he had collected a number of documents diligently and displayed them nicely.

A great reformer and puritan, as he seemed then, he often expressed his deep concern at the degradation of moral values in society, especially in the life of city slickers of that age. As I was his close confidant and had supplied him kilos of *bidis* for his consumption, he told me on a number of occasions about his familiarity with dozens of village belles who lived within a 10-kilometre radius of our village.

He never liked the young blades of our village and lambasted them for being unpunctual. But whenever we went on a fishing expedition, he always came late by at least an hour. Sometimes, to prove his punctuality, he would draw forth an ageing pocket watch from his trouser pocket, which, to our astonishment, generally ran not an hour but two hours late.

My bachelor friend considered himself to be the best angler of the area and gave us numerous lectures on the finer points of fishing. But while we young boys caught a large quantity of fish, he would generally draw a blank. "Why have you not caught any fish, uncle?" we would ask him. And pat would come the reply: "I only catch big fish."

Once we were fishing in the Sarda river. Lady Luck was with me that day, and I caught a big *mahaseer* fish weighing around five kilograms. My heart was filled with joy, and straightaway I ran to him to show off the fish and get his approval. He darted an envious glance at me and after a little while thundered, "Fool, this is a female, I catch only male fish." I was dumbstruck to hear this remark, and found myself almost rooted to the ground. How he could know the sex of the fish would always remain a mystery to me which probably even a marine biologist would find difficult to fathom!

Towards the end of his life, he confessed candidly of his misdeeds, and told me of the high places he had tumbled from and the low places he had tumbled into. So much his concern for "degradation of moral values."

❏❏❏

19

Muktesar's Man-eater

Forty kilometres from the town of Almora via a short cut is a hill, 7500 feet high, 20 kilometres long and running east to west. On this hill exists India's oldest veterinary research institute, built more than a hundred years ago and close to it is the small town of Muktesar. Once, a tigress had established her headquarters in the jungle existing in the vicinity of the institute and begun to live happily there feeding on pigs, porcupines, kakkar, and domestic cattle which are still found in good numbers here. Unfortunately, one day she got badly injured in her encounter with a porcupine. She lost one of her eyes and got fifty quills embedded in her body. This injury forced her to become an established man-eater and she killed more than

24 people. Finally, she fell to the bullet of the legendary Jim Corbett. So I went to Muktesar.

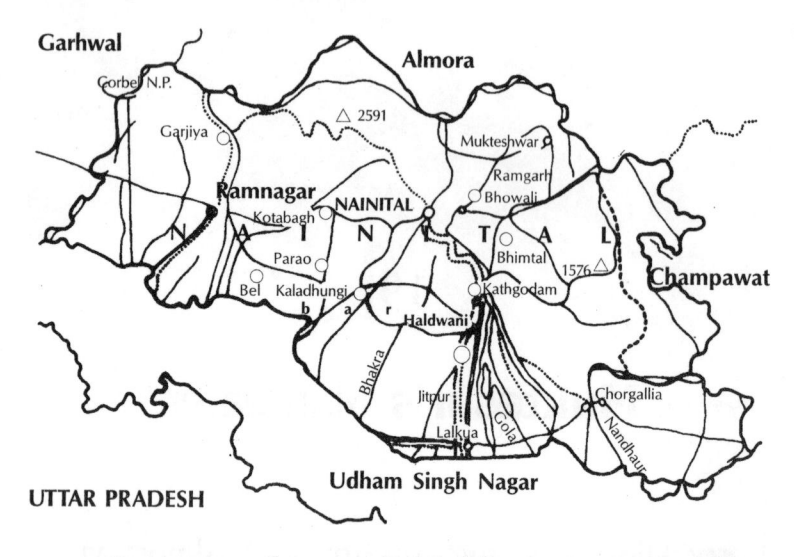

I was on foot and 15 kilometres away from Muktesar when the idea of the man-eater crossed my mind. It requires steely nerves and guts to face a tiger, especially a man-eater, when one is on foot in the forest. However, I reached Muktesar in the afternoon. Call it *kismat* or luck, it plays an important role in one's life. There on the goat track, I chanced to meet Robinson Dass, an ecologist, whose land is close to that of the late Badri Shah. Robinson is familiar with the layout of the land, and took me to where the man-eater had killed her last victim. He showed me that place where the man-eater chased Badri's servant for more than a mile.

Next day, we went down a rugged and steep ridge overgrown with brushwood, beneath which was a deep chasm in which was flowing a rivulet, probably the place where a beat had been carried out. The jungle was dense and overgrown with thorny bushes. The thorns tore through our flesh, and we found some drops of blood on our faces and hands. In the evening we reached the old post office, built in 1905, where the man-eater's skin was placed for the postmaster and villagers. Lastly, Robinson took me to the house of Mrs Chapman, who is more than 90 years old, and the only surviving British lady living in this area.

The post office of Muktesar where the man-eater was brought for public view

The man-eater of Muktesar has withered so has Jim Corbett, but the present writer is still around to tell you this narrative.

20

Mystery of the Yeti

No creature has amazed the biologists of the world so much as the yeti. Now the question that arises is: What is a yeti? Is it a wildman, bearman or a stump-tailed macaque? It is said that this strange creature lives on the higher mountains of Nepal, Tibet and some mountains of China. Some people have given an account of this animal, but there is no similarity in their views.

The mystery of the yeti assumed serious proportion with the discovery of some strange hair by Sir Edmund Hillary during his expedition of Mount Everest. Such hair had never been found in the world. Thus the whole issue stands to close scrutiny and deserves serious consideration.

In China, some 3,000 years old local records and legends still exist about the existence of the yeti or wildman or stump-tailed macaque. Now scientific departments in China have taken up the task to clear the mystery of the yeti and work is going on in this respect.

Some of the projects include the 1959 snowman expedition near the Everest; research into a wildman in Yunnan's Xi Shuang Ban Na forest in 1961; a probe into the report of a strange animal with human appearance in Hubai and Shaanxi; and exploration in Jiulong mountains after reports of a bearman in 1980. The search for the bearman in Jiulong mountains threw light for the first time on the anatomy of the wildman—especially its feet and hands. The investigation found it to be of a stump-tailed macaque.

One of the world's leading authorities on wildman, Zhou Guoxing, made investigations in 1983 and 1984 in the Pamir region about the existence of the wildman. He was surprised to find very old records about the wildman.

His own view was that there was a strange and unknown type of animal with the appearance of a man, and it is not a myth. Its fossils have been found in India and southern China. The discovery of some strange hair by Sir Edmund Hillary gives further credence to the theory that some strange creature exists in the higher ranges of the Himalayas.

According to Zhou Guoxing, there are two types of animals: one is about a metre tall and the second one is more than two metres tall. The footprint of the large one is between 30 and 40 centimetres long.

In appearance, the wildman seems to be a cross between a human and some ape. The ears, hands and the genitals of a male are like that of a man; the female has twin breasts. Its hair are reddish brown and sometimes grey or black. The wildman generally walks upright and goes on all fours while climbing or running fast.

They don't have any language but make monotonous sounds. In his view, many of the wildmen that have been reported so far have turned out to be either monkeys or bears. In 1957, a bearman was killed and its relics were preserved and examined later on. The animal turned out to be a stump-tailed macaque. In 1984, a wildman was reported to have been captured and investigations again proved it to be a stump-tailed macaque.

Due to geological changes, many animals have perished as they could not adapt themselves to the new changes, but some animals like the panda could survive as they changed their habits according to the new requirements. Most reports about the wildman have come from those regions of China which still have some virgin forests. It is a strong possibility that this strange animal too might have changed his habits and still be living in those regions.

❑❑❑

21

Corbett's Brave Companion

The temple of Purnagiri is one of the most famous temples of India where thousands of devotees come from all across the country to pay respect to the goddess Bhagvati. Few years ago, I also visited this temple in the company of Mathura Dutt Pandey, but my objective was to see the mountain on the Nepal side where some strange lights appear. On my way back, *punditji* told me about their native village, Thak, and extracted a promise from me to visit it.

Thak is around 1000 metres above Chuka and was given by the Chand *rajas* to the *pundits* who were appointed custodians of Purnagiri temple. Later on many *pundits*, because of some reasons, settled down in different places leaving it almost deserted.

In November 2, I went to Chuka with great difficulty and after two days, I set off to visit this village in the company of Tirlochan Singh Bhatt, a forest worker. We went across the village and at the edge of the field the path divides, one goat track goes straight up a ridge to Thak, and the other one goes to the village of Kotkindri.

The rock near which the Thak man-eater was shot

The climb was very stiff. Here the forest was very dense and our progress of necessity was very slow. We meandered our way through the rocks, boulders and ravines, Finally, we reached a place thoroughly tired and perspiring. This place was comparatively plain and was covered by small bushes. On the right side of the track, I saw some rocks. It was here that Tirlochan stopped and sat on one of the two black rocks around four feet high. These two rocks are close to each other.

He smiled at me and after lighting his *bidi* said, "*Sahib*, this is the rock from where the man-eater of Thak was shot. And you are the first Indian who has ever come here. Before you only some foreign *sahibs* have come here." On hearing this, I was on the moon. But suddenly in my imaginations, I thought the roaring and charging man-eater on top of me, for nerves wear thin when one roams in such man-eater's terrain. I succeeded in taking the photograph of the rock and returned to the village.

Having taken our dinner, we made a small fire and sat around it. Then an old, frail man named Jeet Singh came all the way from Hera village to meet me. He sat at my feet and said, "*Sahib*, have you seen and taken the photograph of the rock from where a *bagh* (tiger) was shot with two bullets—one hit it on the eye and the other hit it in the neck." I was stunned to hear his correct version. "How do you know this?" I asked him.

Very politely, this unknown and illiterate man said, "One of the four men who was the owner of the goat was my real uncle, Dungar Singh. He stood up and saved Corbett *sahib* from injury when he was falling after firing at the man-eater, which was roaring and was on top of them. Later on, the British government presented my uncle with a gun in recognition of his bravery."

Had Jim Corbett been alive, how happy he would have been to know that the name of his brave companion whose name he forgot to mention in his story of *The Thak Man-eater* has finally been revealed to the world by this writer.

❏❏❏

22

Lights in the Sky

Some years ago, my friend Vinod Rishi of the Indian Forest Service, who has done considerable work in the field of wildlife, came to meet me. Over a cup of coffee, we exchanged our experiences about the mysterious manifestations, sights and sounds in the forest for which we could not give any rational explanation. But they do exist, about this we were quite certain. Jim Corbett, too, has written on three occasions about these inexplicable phenomena which he himself had experienced.

It was in 1962 that I received my first appointment to teach English in a school in the small town of Bhagalpur in Deoria district. The school was on the banks of the Ghagra river. The principal very kindly sent his peon to fetch me from the station. The next day he showed me into a small cottage where I lived during my brief tenure.

The room was small and had remained uninhabited for a long time; it was dark, dingy, and had a musty smell. I spotted a number of bats, not to speak of scorpions which were crawling about on the floor. However, as I was a stranger to the town and couldn't arrange alternative accommodation, I had no other option but to live there.

There was scrub jungle around the cottage where at night I often spotted packs of jackals, wild cats, antelopes, nightjars, and a big owl. In the absence of human company, they naturally became the focus of my attention and source of entertainment.

I had been a week at the place when an extraordinary incident happened which has etched itself indelibly in my memory. It was a dark night; the sky was overcast with thick clouds and lightning flashed sporadically. An eerie silence pervaded the atmosphere, punctuated by the howling of jackals and the hooting of an owl. Suddenly, I saw lights of different colours in the sky. They were red, blue, green, yellow and pink. They hovered about a hundred metres above the ground, and appeared at regular intervals near the banks of the river. I was more fascinated than alarmed. The ethereal show went on for quite some time and ended only when the clouds began to thin out.

As the sun came out the next morning, I went to the spot to satisfy my curiosity. There on the banks of the river, I saw an old *sadhu*. "Do you sometimes see lights in the sky at night?" I asked of him. "Yes, I do," he replied. "In which season do you see them?" I inquired. "Mostly in the months of *sawan* and *bhadu*," he answered. I realised the place was a *shamshan ghat*, a cremation ground. The only explanation which I can offer as to the cause of the strange lights was the presence of phosphorus in the atmosphere, which when it came in direct contact with air currents at a certain altitude, produced light. If readers can advance more plausible explanations, I'd be happy to hear them.

❐❐❐

23

How Green was My Valley!

The Ramganga river, after playing hide and seek with Kanda where Jim Corbett killed the man-eater of Kanda, enters the vale of Kalagarh in the Terai. Many years ago, I went to this river for fishing. Our camp commanded a panoramic view of the lush green valley. The area was bordered on the three sides by the Ramganga river and on the fourth, by the forest dotted over with sal, *sheesham* and *haldu* trees. The valley finally merged with the mountains and there was no trace of human habitation for miles around. At night, one could hear the call of the tiger, leopard, sambhar, kakkar and cheetal. Everyday in the morning and evening, I could see a number of grey partridges moving about our camp and making *'patiloo patiloo'* calls and their fight, which generally took place in the evening, was quite absorbing.

A view of the forest across the Ramganga

One baking hot afternoon, I took an earthen pitcher to fetch water for my camp from a deep pool of cool, crystal clear water. Having filled the pitcher, I sat in a bush to have a soothing smoke and to feast my eyes on the breathtaking view of the valley. On my right flank, I saw a red jungle fowl scratching leaves looking for worms. Occasionally, it would raise its head and finding no danger around, it would lower its head and again scratch the leaves. Soon came a herd of some twenty cheetals but they stood stock still.

Soon a doe gave an alarm call and all the animals took to their heels and the red jungle fowl sailed over the trees. Why the animals had run away was a mystery. As I was pondering over it, I saw a little movement in the bushes behind me. Then I saw the head of a leopard gently projecting from behind a clump of bushes. It was an outsized male leopard. Those who are familiar with our jungles will know that a leopard is incomparable in beauty and grace. In strength and courage, it is second to none.

Since I was in his direct line of vision, he saw me and lay flat on the ground with flattened ears. After a while, he rose gently and began to move towards the pool. On reaching the pool he made a low muttering sound, probably to show his contempt for my presence in the territory which was his. This entire sequence left an indelible print on my memory.

After a lapse of many years, I again went to the place but there was no trace of the lush green valley and the jungle. The entire area was dotted with farmhouses and at night, instead of hearing the call of animals, I heard film songs blaring from transistor sets. If we fail to raise our voice at the depredation of forest and wildlife, our own survival on this planet will soon be in jeopardy.

❏❏❏

24

Poaching Poses Threat to Wildlife

The killing of many tigers by some poachers shows how lopsided and brittle are our steps and measures for the protection of tigers. Though countries like Kenya, Uganda, Botswana, South Africa and Namibia have taken drastic steps to curb poaching, not much has been done in India. In spite of our tall claims, plans and policies, the population of tigers and leopards has reached a red-mark level. If hard and drastic steps are not taken today, India may lose probably one of the most precious parts of its natural heritage.

There are two types of poaching: one done by the local people and the other by professional poachers. In India, the major part of its population, which is poor, lives in villages. To a great extent, the people of the villages depend on the plants, trees, birds and wild animals of their areas. To get meat supply, they kill the animals and the birds. The local poaching, which is done in many parts of India, is done on a low level. Many tribes in India such as *Bheels, Gonds, Kanjars, Haburas, Sansis* and *Bhantus* kill only birds and small animals, such as partridges, doves, pigeons, foxes, jackals and rabbits. Their activities, though illegal and harmful, won't pose very serious problem to the existence of wildlife.

These people kill the birds and small animals by trap (*phanda*). They also use muzzle-loaders, catapults or bows and arrows to kill the birds and small animals. Since these weapons are not very effective, the number of animals or birds killed is not much.

Professional poaching is the worst enemy of wildlife. It is done in an organised way by groups of people armed with modern and sophisticated weapons. Their *modus operandi* is first to know the area where tigers and leopards are found. In this area, they make contacts with some villagers and petty forest officials; some of them are bribed. If a kill takes place in this area, they are informed, and they poison the kill. When the big cat eats the kill, it also dies. They find the kill by its pugmarks. At night, the poachers roam about the forest in jeeps equipped with powerful searchlights. They kill the animals with rifles or guns.

Having killed the big cat, they skin it and take away its bones. On their way back, they hide the skin in the wheel or even in the engine of the vehicle.

Another type of poaching which is confined to Orissa is called *akhand shikar*. Here, during the festival of *Pana Sankranti*, large groups of tribals, sometimes numbering 500 assemble in the forest, flush out the animals and kill them. But now the forest department of Orissa has enlisted the services of the Armed Police Reserve to curb poaching.

Undoubtedly, poaching has assumed alarming proportions in the areas not far from the boundaries of Nepal like the Corbett National Park, Dudhwa and Kaziranga. Scores of leopards, tigers and rhinos are killed every year in these areas which, unfortunately, go unnoticed. Dehradun, Kotdwar, Pithoragarh, Almora, Haldwani, Ramnagar, Moradabad, Rampur and Bareilly are the main centres of poaching. In Thulighat and Pancheswar, one can cross over to Nepal by boat easily, and there is no sign of any policeman for miles around.

Unfortunately, many cases of poaching are still lingering in the courts and because of lack of evidence, most of the poachers are let off the hook. The need of the hour is to create awareness among the villagers and get their cooperation in whose proximity some tigers and leopards are still battling for their survival. If the problem is not addressed today, these beautiful animals may become a part of our museums.

❑❑❑

25

Don't Kill the World...

The declaration of the United Nations to declare the year 2002 as the International Year of Mountains is a step in the right direction. Mountains and forests are not only the home of bio-diversity but also of thousands of rivers which quench the thirst of millions of people, all across the globe. They are home to communities worldwide and to important cultural traditions. Similarly, the role of the forests for global environment can never be overlooked. According to Klaus Toepfer, the executive director of the UN Environment Programme, "Forests contain some of the most vibrant ecosystems on the planet, they are home to a wondrous variety of birds, animals, insects and plants. Forests provide fuel, materials for building, natural medicines and foods such as nuts and berries. They also play a critical role in regulating river flows and—by soaking up carbon dioxide from the atmosphere—the climate."

Depleted forests of the Himalayas

However, man, in his greed to make quick money, is destroying the ecosystem, especially forests and mountains which is having adverse effect on our climate. According to the International Centre for Integrated Mountain Development, 44 glacial lakes in Nepal and Bhutan now contain hazardous levels of water due to global warming melting the nearby glaciers.

After various research and studies conducted by United Nations, some hard facts have emerged which are indeed pathbreaking and worth noting.

According to the report, over 70 per cent of the earth's land surface could be affected by the impact of roads, mining, cities, and other infrastructure developments in the next 30 years. Around 75 per cent of Latin America, the Caribbean region, Asia and Pacific regions will be affected by habitat disturbances and other kinds of environmental damage. Similarly, more than half the people in the world, especially of the Arabian Peninsula, could be living in severely water stressed areas by 2032 if the market forces drive the globe's political, economic and social agenda. The report further points out that the number of people affected by disasters climbed from an average of 147 million a year in the 1980s to 211 million a year in the 1990s. Natural disasters in 1990 cost global financial losses to the tune of US$ 100 billion.

Half of the world's rivers are seriously depleted and polluted. Around 60 per cent of the world's largest 227 rivers have been strongly or moderately fragmented by dams and other engineering works. Furthermore, it is estimated that forests which cover a third of the earth's land surface have declined by 2.4 per cent since 1990. Mangrove forests, natural sea defences, nursery grounds for fish and nesting sites for migratory birds are threatened. Twelve percent or 1,183 of birds and nearly a quarter of

1,130 mammals are currently regarded as globally threatened.

The condition of our forests growing at the foothills of the Himalayas is dismal. Almost a 100 years ago, our forests were lush green where grew sal, *sheesham*, *banjh*, deodar trees, and a number of medicinal plants. These forests have become almost depleted as people living in the surrounding villages are cutting them for fodder and fuel wood. The results are appalling: some small rivers and springs which were the main source of water supply to the villages have dried up or flow in a trickle. Similarly, pink duck and the Himalayan quail have become extinct, and tiger, leopard, musk deer, Manipur deer and some other species have reached the red-mark level. Human race is at a crossroads. If we fail to read the writings on the wall, it is possible that we may be annihilated by some gigantic calamity as happened in the days of Noah and described in the Bible.

❐❐❐

26

King Bandit

About 50 miles from my town and in the thick jungle lived Sultana, who was considered to be one of the greatest bandits that has ever lived in India. He spent some parts of his early childhood under the care of Salvation Army Mission, at Moradabad. Unfortunately, he could not mend his ways, and became a bandit.

Soon he became so powerful that once he had a gang of around a hundred armed bandits at his command, and operated in northern India. But he was so magnanimous that once he spared the life of the legendary Jim Corbett in the jungle, else the world would not have known anything about Corbett and the man-eaters of Kumaon.

In those bygone days, my house was on the edge of the forest, and fairly close to my house lived an old pastor named Bailey. He was the only person in the area who knew Sultana personally and commanded his respect, much to the displeasure and discomfort of the people in power. But the old pastor did not budge an inch from his moral grounds and loved Sultana. He was a frequent visitor to our house and told us about his personal meetings and experiences with Sultana.

One evening, over a cup of tea, he told us that once two Europeans came to Bijnor on a shooting expedition, and stayed in the bungalow of an American lady. On a crisp clear day, they headed for the forest. On entering the forest, they soon found themselves encircled by a gang of armed dacoits. Out came Sultana and ordered them to surrender their guns, and asked them to return to their country.

The news of the incident caught on like wildfire, creating a tumult of commotion and excitement in the area. Soon Bailey was summoned and sent to broker a deal with Sultana. Bailey prevailed upon Sultana and requested him to return the guns. After three or four days, the guns were found in the compound with a note written in Urdu which read as follows: "I have never killed anyone in my life, nor have I robbed a poor man.

But the British police is after my blood. I want to see my India as a free country". After few years, Sultana was nabbed in the forest while he was fast asleep, and sentenced to death on insubstantial and false charges. Though he was a bandit, his heart bled for his country.

❏❏❏

27

Tigers of **Talla Des**

Since my childhood, it had always been my burning ambition to see, photograph, and to write about those exact spots where the legendary Jim Corbett shot man-eaters that once established a reign of terror in those farflung areas which are still away from the din and buzz of modern civilisation. It was a Herculean and arduous task, as I was alone with no support from any quarters whatsoever. However, success came only through hard work and perseverance. As I had been to Chuka, Thak, Champawat and Kanda, so it was time to set off to Talla Des where two sleeping tigers had been shot from a *wyran* (deserted) field.

I had informed *pundit* Purshotam Joshi, who has been a block *pramukh* of this area for many years, about the date of my visit. It was a raw evening when I reached his house in Tamli village. During the course of our talk, he brought to light many facts, including the brave deeds of the people of this area, which had gone unnoticed in the annals of wildlife. Next day, taking the good wishes of my friend, I set out for village Thola Kot, which is around 12 kilometres away. On reaching Thola Kot, I was welcomed by none other than Sundar Singh, the grandson of the brave Dungar Singh. Soon he placed food for me on an improvised table. After satisfying the inner man, I asked him about the *wyran* field where two sleeping tigers had been killed. Sundar Singh along with his two

Wyran field on which two tigers cubs accompanying the man-eater, were shot

brothers took me to a goat track which starts from the saddle of the village. We had gone for about three hundred metres where the track divides—one track goes deep into the ravine where Dungar Singh's mother had been eaten by the tigers, while the other track goes up to the crest of the ridge.

This right track leads to a field, around hundred metres long, which has gone out of cultivation because of lack of water. This field goes steep down and turns to the left. At the end is a chasm, many metres deep. From this spot, Sundar Singh pointed out towards the *wyran* field where the two tigers were sleeping in sunshine. He said that the tiger which was farther away was shot first, then the nearer one. Both the tigers dropped dead. There was also a third tiger, and a bullet was fired at it, injuring it badly. It was shot after some days. "Where was the third tiger shot?" I asked him. Sundar Singh took me to the other side of the village across the cultivated land. From the edge of the field, which gave a commanding view of the valley below, he pointed to a place surrounded by pine trees where the third tiger, a tigress and the real man-eater, was shot.

Though the three tigers of Thola Kot have been shot, the *wyran* field of Thola Kot remains untouched from the ravages of time.

28

Braving a Bear Attack

India is a large country, and home to hundreds of animals. But some animals like leopards, tigers and bears, though dwindling in numbers, cause concern, especially, in the areas adjoining their habitats. The reason is apparent: they sometimes attack, injure and even kill human beings.

In India, brown and black bears are found in the higher ranges of the Himalayas. Brown bear is becoming scarce. The big male may measure over seven feet from nose to the root of the tail and may weigh around 400 lbs. It spends most of its time in the higher levels, well above the tree-line.

As a rule, black bears are vegetarians; they eat fruit, berries, leaves, grass and honey but also birds' eggs, small animals and termites. On a number of occasions, they walk up to the feeding leopards and after shooing them off, carry their kills and eat it.

Now the question that crops up is: Why do the black bears attack, injure and sometimes kill human beings when human beings don't form a part of their diet? After detailed studies, it has been found that in most of the attacks, it is the male which attacks and injures human beings without being provoked. Females attack human beings only when they think their young ones are threatened.

In Champawat, I came across a woman who had been attacked by a bear. One eyeball came out of the socket; her nose was chopped off; and she received severe injuries on her throat and upper parts of her breast. Dr Karnataka, an eminent surgeon of Champawat, after initial treatment sent her to Lucknow. She became all right after eight months. Devki, a native of Pithoragarh district, was attacked by a bear. She received facial injuries, lost her lower eyelids, a portion of the nose and cheeks. She came to Delhi and received treatment for three weeks from Dr P S Bhandari, a competent and dedicated plastic surgeon.

Dr Bhandari pointed out that because of lack of basic medical facilities at the village level, the patient may lose considerable amount of blood and may succumb to injuries. He further said that painkillers, proper dressing material, and broad-spectrum antibiotics should be made available in bear-infested areas. "Our poor village folk know very little about plastic surgery. If they lose their nose, ear and lips in bear attacks, it can be reconstructed to its perfection with advanced plastic surgical procedures," he remarked during my chat.

❏❏❏

29

Jungle Laws are Eternal and True

Unfortunately, many politicians, intellectuals and bureaucrats use the phrase 'Jungle Raj' without knowing the true meaning of it. The jungle law is eternal and the the oldest law in the world, and came into being much before man made his appearance on this planet. It is as perfect as time and custom can make it. Had we followed some of its laws, there would have been peace on this planet.

The first law of the jungle is that all animals and birds, big or small, respect man and keep themselves at a safe distance. Some big cats like lions, tigers and leopards, attack and kill man when their food gets scarce, their habitats destroyed, they get old and crippled and their cubs are threatened.

Animals are afraid of the elephant, bear, tiger, lion, leopard, crocodile, python and dragon. Never will they disturb these animals and reptiles, instead, they go away from their presence.

Animals never fight for grazing rights

Everything in the forest has a particular function to discharge which it does with regularity and consistency. The trees give oxygen and food to the birds and animals; the birds make their nests in the trees and animals stay under them for shade. The grass and shrubs also provide food to the animals and birds. The herbivores eat grass and leaves and help to keep a check on the growth of the forest. Carnivores eat the animals to keep a check on their growth. Many years ago, some settlers in Australia got some rabbits from England, but, since there was no carnivore in Australia, the population of rabbits multiplied manifold and they became a serious threat to the Australian continent. Similarly, red deer were transported to New Zealand from Europe and they increased so fast in the absence of any carnivore that many of the red deer were ordered to be shot in order to keep their population in check. The birds eat insects and rodents and the snakes eat other snakes and rodents. Thus, all animals and birds keep a balance in nature.

Nothing goes waste in the jungle. The leaves, fruits and berries when they fall from the trees serve as manure to the trees; when an animal gets old, sick or crippled, it is eaten by other animals like hyenas, dogs or jackals. When some chicks of the birds die, they are eaten away by crows, kites or falcons. Some birds of the falcon family finding their chicks dead, feed them to the living chicks.

Among the birds and animals that live in flocks and herds, it is the strongest male which has the right to produce the offspring, because in nature it is the strongest that can survive. When two males fight, the herd keeps itself away from the fight, else the entire herd may be wiped out.

Animals of the forest never fight for grazing rights. They feed together peacefully. They also share food with other animals. Monkeys, langurs and birds drop fruit and berries from the trees which are picked up by other animals from the ground and eaten. Sensing danger, some animals give an alarm call and other animals immediately run for safety.

In the jungles, there is a time of cease-fire when no killing takes place. This time is from around 10 pm to 3 am. During this time, the killer and the prey sleep peacefully. There may be a little variation in the time depending on the position of the moon and stars.

During the time of any natural calamity, like fire, quake or flood, animals do not fight or kill one another; they run for safety and there is no killing. Killing is done when the calamity is over.

Mighty animals like lions and tigers never kill the very young and defenceless of other species. Once, a tigress saw a small kid in the forest and the kid also saw the tigress. The tigress met the kid nose to nose, but soon returned the way she had come. She did not kill the kid, for she was the queen of the forest and it would have been an insult to her to have killed the kid.

❏❏❏

30

Saluting Some Unsung Jungle Heroes

After roaming the jungles of India, especially of Garhwal and Kumaon for more than 40 years, I have reached this firm conviction that the hill folk of these regions are the sturdiest and the simplest in India, and in bravery, they are second to none; for the soldiers of the Garhwal and Kumaon regiments had won many bravery awards, including Victoria Crosses, in the last two World Wars. However, my tryst with destiny will be incomplete if I fail to give a brief account of one of my late and brave jungle companions.

The night was closing in when I reached the village of Thola Kot, absolutely bone tired and hungry that day. The first man to come out to greet me was none other than Sundar Singh, the grandson of Dungar Singh whose mother had been killed by the man-eater of Talla Des, many years ago.

"What is your name?" I asked him.

"My name is Sundar Singh. I am the grandson of Dungar Singh."

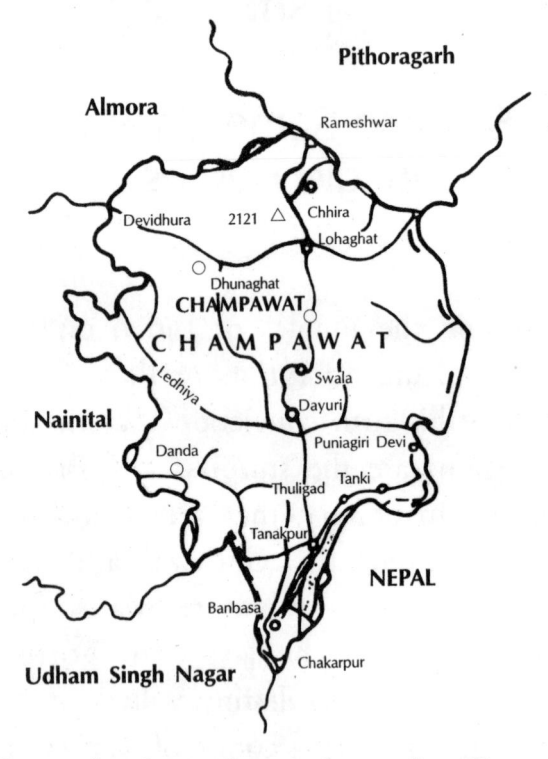

[Map showing the Champawat region with locations including Almora, Pithoragarh, Rameshwar, Devidhura, Chhira, Lohaghat, Dhunaghat, Champawat, Ledhiya, Swala, Dayuri, Nainital, Danda, Puniagiri Devi, Thuligad, Tanki, Tanakpur, Banbasa, Nepal, Udham Singh Nagar, Chakarpur]

Soon, he brought a glass of milk sweetened with *gur*—a pleasant drink if one gets accustomed to it. He made a roaring fire, and we sat around it chatting and smoking. Our hill folk are probably the most hospitable people in the world. They rely on an outsider, which is a rare phenomenon and possible only in India. Sundar Singh's left hand and elbow was twisted and bent. "Why is your hand twisted?" I asked him. "You know *sahib*, bears are found in large numbers here. One day, as I was cutting grass, a bear came and attacked me. In the fight that ensued, the bear broke my elbow. I applied *haldi* and *choona* and bandaged my hand. I got all right after some months. I am an unlucky person. After some months, a wild boar attacked me from behind and chewed my wrist." Though poor and working only with one hand, my friend made me comfortable in his small hut. The life of this lonely and poor man touched the core of my heart, and taught me how to lead an honest life and do brave deeds. Unfortunately, their names are blank in the pages of history.

Sundar Singh had a passion for wildlife and ecology and knew more of it than some of us who champion it for power, pelf and position. He now has been summoned into another world where I, too, will join him one day.

Many years ago, I was trekking the Lohaghat valley. It was a blasting cold morning when I reached a small tea stall by the roadside. Inside the stall, I found five village folk seated around a small fire. As I reached it, one man came out and saluted me with his left hand for he had only one hand. There was some thing unusual about him and I began to look at him with amusing curiosity. He was a happy-go-lucky man, tall in stature and decidedly small in circumference, had a pair of shining eyes twinkling with mirth and merriment. He had an air of chivalry about him which was quite intimidating. Hereafter, he began to sing a folk song to the immeasurable delight of this small group, occasionally winking to them. I, too, could not help smiling. As the conversation developed, he told me he had lost his hand in 1948 while fighting against the marauders who invaded Kashmir.

Sundar Singh of Thola Kot

"Are you happy with your lot?" I inquired of him. "You know *sahib*, my home is here; I love my jungles and my hills. I have shared these happy moments with you, for I will not see you again." These words touched the core my heart.

Now it was time for me to make a move, for my destination was still far away. The poor brave man came all the way to show me the way. At the time of final parting, he stuffed the only packet of cigarette he was carrying into my pocket in spite of my protestation. (In those days, I was a smoker).

These brave people of the hills, who fought so valiantly for the protection of our country, some of them now crippled and disabled, would wither away one day. But by their brave deeds, they have made our country a nation of the brave.

Vaibhav